Poetry For a Change

A NATIONAL POETRY DAY ANTHOLOGY

Text copyright © the individual poets 2018

Illustrations copyright © Chie Hosaka 2018

First published in Great Britain in 2018 by
Otter-Barry Books, Little Orchard, Burley Gate, Herefordshire, HR1 3QS
www.otterbarrybooks.com
in association with Forward Arts Foundation, organisers of
National Poetry Day

ISBN 978-1-910959-50-3

Illustrated with dip pen and ink, calligraphy brush and pencil

Set in Garamond Premier Pro and ITC Avant Garde Gothic

Printed in the United Kingdom

9 8 7 6 5 4 3 2 1

Poetry
For a Change

A NATIONAL
POETRY DAY
ANTHOLOGY

Illustrated by Chie Hosaka

Otter-Barry BOOKS

Contents

Introduction

Welcome to the first ever Poetry For a Change anthology. This book contains 43 poems – more than half are freshly written by living, breathing poets, the rest include classics that they want to share with you, by writers as various as Emily Dickinson, Yeats and that playful shape-shifter Anon.

The theme of change threads through them all, and though you will spot recurring subjects – the seasons, seeds, time – we hope you will also be jolted into laughter and surprise by poems which change as you read them.

There are werewolves stalking these pages, chameleons and caterpillars; sunflowers, snapshots and summer holidays. Some poems are like changing rooms: you go in as one person and come out as another, with a new voice, an extra joke, intimate knowledge of ancient names for the phases of the moon.

This book will be useful at any time of year, but may be particularly valuable in the run-up, or aftermath, of National Poetry Day in October, when seeking poems to pin on walls, to copy and share – and to spark off new poems in the fizzing brains of young readers, writers and performers.

We have included some handy tips at the back of this book, but you will find more on www.nationalpoetryday.co.uk, a site with links to many ideas, images, poems and recommended reading.

Finally, from the team at Forward Arts Foundation, the charity that organises National Poetry Day, here's a poem by Imtiaz Dharker. We love it for showing how we all change – our manner, our words, our expressions – on crossing the threshold between home and the outside world. It will conjure up different images and sounds in all who read it. List them, write them down, sing them out.

It's poetry, for a change.

Susannah Herbert
Director, National Poetry Day and the Forward Arts Foundation
www.nationalpoetryday.co.uk

Front Door

by Imtiaz Dharker

Wherever I have lived,
walking out of the front door
every morning
means crossing over
to a foreign country.

One language inside the house,
another out.
The food and clothes
and customs change.
The fingers on my hand turn
into forks.

I call it adaptation
when my tongue switches
from one grammar to another,
but the truth is I'm addicted now,
high on the rush
of daily displacement,
speeding to a different time zone,
heading into altered weather,
landing as another person.

Don't think I haven't noticed
you're on the same trip too.

With kind permission of the author and Bloodaxe Books.

Deborah Alma

Spring

Not a small thing, it is
a look to the left to see

a hawthorn hedge
flaring its flowers

and a tiny bird step up to the edge
of the nest for the first time,

as it hops from one thorny stem,
to another, uncertain and then

in a small fluster,
the lift of it –

the marvel and magic of it
in love with itself –

with what it can suddenly do.

Deborah Alma writes:
This little poem is about the baby bird for the first time finding out
what it was born to do, and although it's about a little bird, it's also
about you. (Apart from the actual flying – don't try that part. This is a
metaphor!)

My second choice is an old proverb-poem, so old that no one remembers who wrote it and so it's by Anonymous (or Anon for short). I love this idea that changing one small thing can have such a big effect... It is also a metaphor for how we can make big changes in the world from our small actions.

For Want of a Nail

For want of a nail the shoe was lost.
For want of a shoe the horse was lost.
For want of a horse the rider was lost.
For want of a rider the battle was lost.
For want of a battle the kingdom was lost.
And all for the want of a horseshoe nail.

Anon

Liz Brownlee

Snow Fox

In the Arctic summer
the cloud-grey fox
listens for prey
in the low shrubs and rocks

grizzled and still
as the permafrost ground
his senses vivid
with scent and sound

when lemmings are hidden
under the snow
the wild geese are flown
and biting winds blow

a horizon-less white
shrouds the Arctic fox
in clouds of snow fur
from tail-tip to socks

he haunts frozen sea
as thin as the air
hoping for scraps
missed by polar bear

or curls in his tail
from the star-cold white
chewing on hunger
through long Arctic night

and waits for spring sun
and pale Arctic day
to melt tundra snow
and his white coat away

Liz Brownlee writes:
How does the fox's fur knows when it is time to change from
grey-brown to white in the winter, and back again in the spring?
I love the fact that we don't really know, and it's the inspiration
for my poem.

It's why I've chosen to pair it with *Something Told the Wild Geese*
by Rachel Field. She wonders what mysterious message tells the
wild birds, especially those hatched that year, that it is time to fly,
and where.

Something Told the Wild Geese

Something told the wild geese
  It was time to go.
Though the fields lay golden
  Something whispered,—'Snow.'
Leaves were green and stirring,
  Berries, luster-glossed,
But beneath warm feathers
  Something cautioned,—'Frost.'
All the sagging orchards
  Steamed with amber spice,
But each wild breast stiffened
  At remembered ice.
Something told the wild geese
  It was time to fly,—
Summer sun was on their wings,
  Winter in their cry.

Rachel Field (1894-1942)

John Canfield

He Thinks of his Past Faces

When I was growing up I had a trait,
every time a camera was produced
to take a family snap: I'd stand up straight,
then cheeks and lips and tongue were quickly loosed

into a silly face, a gurn; my eyes
rolled in to both point at my wrinkled nose;
I skewed the angle of my lips, gave size
to my young cheeks, inflating them; up rose

one eyebrow, while one went the other way,
and all of this I'd do in seconds flat.
My mum would see, and turn to me to say,
'If the wind changes, your face will stay like that.'

I've just looked in a mirror, and I saw
a face I find it hard to recognise.
It's not the same as what was there before,
a different phizog, much to my surprise,

to what grins out at me in photographs,
which still is twisted in a comic gurn;
the younger me looks at them and he laughs,
the older me is quite intrigued to learn

my mum's advice would have been accurate
if when a camera came out, she'd said, 'When
the shutter clicks, your face will stay like that
in all these photographs.' If I'd known then

what I know now, I would still make a strange
and silly look appear; for it's the pace
of life and time and how we must face change,
and not the wind, that makes us change our face.

John Canfield writes:
Growing up, I liked showing off and messing around, so in most of
the childhood photographs of me I'm pulling funny faces. I was
looking through some of them recently and it inspired a mixture
of feelings about how I looked and behaved then and now, and
the faces we present to the world. It's more complicated now with
cameras everywhere and I think there's a danger that we can
become too concerned with what we look like in photos rather
than enjoying ourselves and being in the moment. The title of my
poem jokily refers to *He Thinks of His Past Greatness When a Part of
the Constellations of Heaven* by W.B. Yeats, a poem I love, about
someone reflecting on how they've changed throughout their life.
So, this poem came out of those thoughts, and as a reminder to
myself to pull funny faces every now and then.

I have chosen another poem to share with you, by Dora Greenwell, a Victorian poet who campaigned for women's suffrage. As humans, not only do we experience change around us, but we often wish for change in the world and in ourselves; how we look and where we are. Have you ever stared out of the window and daydreamed about being somewhere else? I love the journey this poem takes us on, imagining the freedom of animals, of flowers and thunder, then going up hills and around the world, before coming back to the poet's room. The rhyming couplets sweep us along and the way the sentences run on from line to line give it so much energy. 'Scherzo' is a musical term that means 'quickly moving and playful', which this poem definitely is. It's fun to read, but also thoughtful and moving about what it's like to be human.

A Scherzo

(A Shy Person's Wishes)

With the wasp at the innermost heart of a peach,
On a sunny wall out of tip-toe reach,
With the trout in the darkest summer pool,
With the fern-seed clinging behind its cool
Smooth frond, in the chink of an aged tree,
In the woodbine's horn with the drunken bee,
With the mouse in its nest in a furrow old,
With the chrysalis wrapt in its gauzy fold;
With things that are hidden, and safe, and bold,
With things that are timid, and shy, and free,
Wishing to be;
With the nut in its shell, with the seed in its pod,
With the corn as it sprouts in the kindly clod,

17

Far down where the secret of beauty shows
In the bulb of the tulip, before it blows;
With things that are rooted, and firm, and deep,
Quiet to lie, and dreamless to sleep;
With things that are chainless, and tameless, and proud,
With the fire in the jagged thunder-cloud,
With the wind in its sleep, with the wind in its waking,
With the drops that go to the rainbow's making,
Wishing to be with the light leaves shaking,
Or stones on some desolate highway breaking;
Far up on the hills, where no foot surprises
The dew as it falls, or the dust as it rises;
To be couched with the beast in its torrid lair,
Or drifting on ice with the polar bear,
With the weaver at work at his quiet loom;
Anywhere, anywhere, out of this room!

Dora Greenwell (1821–1882)

Joseph Coelho

Secret Eating

The first nibble of the secret
was tasteless,
like a burnt chip of ice.

I pressed my teeth into the very corner,
felt the satisfying hiss and crack
as the secret gave way.

The secret crumbled,
just-baked-hot, unthawed-freezer-cold,
in my cavity-free mouth.

The secret snowballed there,
threatened to lava-vomit out,
promising to be swallowed down.

The secret's cold syrup skied over my tongue,
a hot taste that masks all flavours,
bathed my teeth until they hurt.

I swallowed –
felt the secret's small charred lump
hail down into my belly and grow.

I carried the secret's meltwater
in my sloshing stomach –
scared its eruption would burn.

The secret's ash clouds stung my eyes,
its freeze numbed my belly,
made my teeth chatter.

You asked about my secret
with sunny breeze eyes
and a dappled shade smile.

I felt the secret quake,
felt its snow storm swirl,
I opened my chattering teeth,

watched the secret puff out of me,
a snowflake in warm air,
watched its mist disappear,

felt my stomach smile,
felt my mouth laugh,
breathed in the toasty warmth of your hug.

Joseph Coelho writes:

Secret Eating grew out of the idea that we can swallow our emotions. It's an attempt to describe what that can feel like. Having a secret that we're too afraid to share can be a horrible experience and one that unfortunately many of us must go through at some time or another. There is a saying that a problem shared is a problem halved, which I thoroughly believe. Through this poem I wanted to track the change that can occur when we share our problems and our secrets, when we go from feeling utterly alone in the world to supported and free.

And for my other poem I'd like to choose *The Seedling* by Paul Laurence Dunbar. Learning about seeds and how they erupt into plants is one of the ways that many of us learn about change from an early age. I've visited countless schools where pots of soil line the window sills as part of projects on growth and change.

I very much enjoy gardening. I love planting seeds in spring and reaping their fruit in autumn and watching them change in the time between. Seedlings are a wonderful metaphor for change and Paul Laurence Dunbar beautifully charts that growth.

The Seedling

As a quiet little seedling
Lay within its darksome bed,
To itself it fell a–talking,
And this is what it said:

"I am not so very robust,
But I'll do the best I can;"
And the seedling from that moment
Its work of life began.

So it pushed a little leaflet
Up into the light of day,
To examine the surroundings
And show the rest the way.

The leaflet liked the prospect,
So it called its brother, Stem;
Then two other leaflets heard it,
And quickly followed them.

To be sure, the haste and hurry
Made the seedling sweat and pant;
But almost before it knew it
It found itself a plant.

The sunshine poured upon it,
And the clouds they gave a shower;
And the little plant kept growing
Till it found itself a flower.

Little folks, be like the seedling,
Always do the best you can;
Every child must share life's labor
Just as well as every man.

And the sun and showers will help you
Through the lonesome, struggling hours,
Till you raise to light and beauty
Virtue's fair, unfading flowers.

Paul Laurence Dunbar (1872-1906)

Sally Crabtree

Changing Room

There's a curtain at the back
    Of your mind
Step behind it
  and
Change!

Your shoes leave such sad footprints
And the worries you wear
Are so threadbare

Let me bring you something new.

Some platforms perhaps?
So high
You can step right onto Heaven's dance floor

And a feather boa or a scarf
Made out of lightness like laughter,
So ticklish
you'll smile at every step

You'll need an outfit with pockets deep enough to hold
the ocean and a bag in which to keep your new *id*.
The new you.

You look wonderful!
Come out
Have a twirl in front of the mirror. Don't be shy
There are all sorts here, trying things on.

The sky looks stunning in that blue
But maybe she'll change into the little black number
Covered in stars
Or the dress where suns rise endlessly from the hem
For her to wear as brooches, spinning...

A violet seedling is trying on a purple shirt.
It goes so well with his green trousers.
His shyness drops like a pearl of dew

A tiny caterpillar's
about to crawl away.
"I haven't got the courage to wear wings," he says.
"Come on," encourages the sky, taking them from the hanger.
"I'll catch you if you fly!"
The good news is there's a SALE on.
Everything is free!
This fashion designer's out of this world

And only wants for you to know how fabulous
you are – darling. So go on,
Choose an outfit. Step behind the curtain
and
Change!

Sally Crabtree writes:
I was inspired to write my poem after reading a line by Hafiz that
said, "Change rooms in your mind for a day." It reminded me of a
great TV programme from our childhood called *Mr Benn*, where a
city gent in a bowler hat would go into a costume shop, change
into an amazing character and go off on an adventure. I do believe
our lives can be an amazing adventure if we dare to just go behind
the curtain in our mind and change! Easier said than done of course
but wonderful to be helped along the way by great poets such as
Hafiz and Omar Khayyam – and of course *Mr Benn*!

I love the almost mystical changing of the light at dawn and these lines from the Rubaiyat of Omar Khayyam have a flavour of this mystery for me. There is also an added mystery as to whether or not the poet actually wrote the lines or whether the translator just added them in! I don't mind who it was – the imagery is a delight either way. In this case, it makes reference to a tradition in the desert where, if the camp was about to change and move on, a stone would be thrown into a cup.

Awake! for Morning in the Bowl of Night
Has flung the Stone that puts the Stars to Flight:
And Lo! the Hunter of the East has caught
The Sultan's Turret in a Noose of Light.

from The Rubaiyat of Omar Khayyam (1048–1131)
Translated by Edward FitzGerald (1809–1883)

Jan Dean

Becoming the Eagle

first came the rash –
not splotchy measle-blotchy
but pinprick neat and pimply
red-pink dots like tiny islands
rising in a sea of skin

next the itch
compelled the scratch
the rake of fingerclaws in flesh
my spine and shoulder blades
against the doorframe
I strained and scraped
but then

the itch inside my head
said *mountainside*
so on the rocks I scoured
my scarlet gooseflesh surface
till it was torn away
and I was all new feathered

none of this was easy
none of this was comfortable
nor was the hollowing of my bones
which made me easy meat
for wild winds while I learned
to slant and angle in the crevice of the gale

hear how it howls my name
and hear my answer cried out
in a tongue I have not learned
to speak

Jan Dean writes:
When I think of how I've changed over my lifetime I see that some
changes have been easier than others and that sometimes changes
which turned out well didn't look as if they were going to turn out
well at all. I chose to write about the unlikely transformation of
a person into an eagle so that I could play with the idea of the
discomfort of change. I liked the idea of showing upset and stress
not as things that happen in your head, but as bodily things. I enjoy
metaphors.

My choice as companion poem is *Ariel's Song* from William
Shakepeare's *The Tempest*, because it presents physical change in
beautiful magical language. It is about the way a drowned body
has become part of the sea, but it is not a gruesome or morbid
poem, it's more like the idea of dinosaurs becoming fossils than an
episode of CSI. I heard it first when I was about ten and I've never
forgotten it. It is absolutely beautiful.

Ariel's Song

Full fathom five thy father lies,
Of his bones are coral made:
Those are pearls that were his eyes,
Nothing of him that doth fade,
But doth suffer a sea-change
Into something rich and strange:
Sea-nymphs hourly ring his knell –
Ding-dong.
Hark! Now I hear them,
Ding-dong bell.

William Shakespeare (1564-1616)

Marjorie Lotfi Gill

Sunflower

Her grandfather always said
that everything she'd need
was beneath the grey of its shell;
the signposts of winter would come
from its height, the strength
of its spine, how long it resisted
before nodding its head to wind.

When she left, she took nothing
but the seeds, their rattle in the tiny
tin better than money; no one else
would know the shade of soil
for planting, want flocks of birds
for friends. Now, she sleeps with them
under her pillow where they grow
into her dreams, stakes to lean against
on each crossing, and wakes
picking at yellow petals
tangled in her hair.

Marjorie Lotfi Gill writes:
When people find out I left Iran as a child during the Iranian
Revolution, we often end up talking about what I took with me on
the journey to America. This poem was written with that question in
mind – why we take things with us if we leave a place we think of
as home, what they remind us of, and what use they are in the new
places where we settle.

I chose this poem by Emily Dickinson to accompany mine because although *Sunflower* is about sunflower seeds, it is also about the potential for change, how we can't control its timing or know what it will bring with it, how sometimes the possibility of change is what gives us strength. In *Dear March – Come in –* the speaker is equally delighted and flustered by March's arrival, having waited so long for that change that she doesn't anticipate the arrival of April!

Dear March - Come in -

Dear March - Come in -
How glad I am -
I hoped for you before -
Put down your Hat -
You must have walked -
How out of Breath you are -
Dear March, how are you, and the Rest -
Did you leave Nature well -
Oh March, Come right upstairs with me -
I have so much to tell -

I got your Letter, and the Birds -
The Maples never knew that you were coming -
I declare - how Red their Faces grew -
But March, forgive me -
And all those Hills you left for me to Hue -
There was no Purple suitable -
You took it all with you -

Who knocks? That April -
Lock the Door -
I will not be pursued -
He stayed away a Year to call
When I am occupied -
But trifles look so trivial
As soon as you have come

That blame is just as dear as Praise
And Praise as mere as Blame -

Emily Dickinson (1830–1886)

33

Chrissie Gittins

The Dilruba Player and the Boy

A blind musician plays the dilruba,
sad sounds come from the strings.

A boy in a wheelchair appears in the audience,
his chest is congested – he wheezes and cries.

He cries and he wails –
the musician can hear him.

Moving his bow over the strings
he echoes the cries of the boy.

The boy cries once more, the musician replies,
the boy silently smiles.

Chrissie Gittins writes:
I attended a *Hear it Live!* session at the Horniman Museum, London,
with Baluji Shrivastav. He played the Dilruba – a stringed instrument
of North India and Pakistan. The poem records a moment during
the performance when the music changed the atmosphere in the
room, and the responses of a particular member of the audience.
'Dilruba' is a Persian word meaning 'heart stealer'.

I chose the companion poem as it's very difficult to write something memorable and captivating in just two lines. I think it encapsulates beautifully the change from our daytime world when we are all together, to our night-time world when we have individual dreams. 'Several' in the sense that it is used here means 'distinct, unique, apart from others'.

Robert Herrick was an English poet and clergyman. His 83 years stretched from Elizabethan times when Shakespeare was writing, to the Restoration period. He wrote over 2,000 poems, some of which were for women who may or may not have been real.

Dreams

Here we all are, by day; by night we're hurled
By dreams, each one, into a several world.

Robert Herrick (1591-1674)

Matt Goodfellow

Chameleon Kids

chameleon kids are elusive
their skill is to rarely be found
drifting through days undetected
blending with those they're around

chameleon kids are careful
their secrets are never revealed
camouflage acting as armour
means feelings are safely concealed

some of them yearn to burn brightly
but predators lurk everywhere
so they learn to disguise any fire in their eyes
until not even they know it's there

Matt Goodfellow writes:
I had lots of different ideas about how to approach the theme of
'Change', but my mind kept coming back to how we as humans
sometimes change to suit the different environments we encounter.
As a primary teacher and a writer in schools, I often meet children
who struggle to 'fit in' and who feel the need to try to change
who they are in order to conform to the 'norm' or, as in my poem,
disappear from view entirely. These are children who need support,
encouragement and kindness in recognising their unique qualities
and individuality – the 'fire in their eyes'.

I've always been fascinated by how nature continues apace as generation after generation of humans come and go. In my companion poem Thomas Hardy thinks about the human body changing after death and becoming part of nature.

Transformations

Portion of this yew
Is a man my grandsire knew,
Bosomed here at its foot:
This branch may be his wife,
A ruddy human life
Now turned to a green shoot.

These grasses must be made
Of her who often prayed,
Last century, for repose;
And the fair girl long ago
Whom I often tried to know
May be entering this rose.

So, they are not underground,
But as nerves and veins abound
In the growths of upper air,
And they feel the sun and rain,
And the energy again
That made them what they were!

Thomas Hardy (1840-1928)

Remi Graves

Portobello's Soul

I walk down my street
to find the soul of the place
looking for a space to land.

I see it first way up high
flapping through yawning clouds
trying not to hit the

red eyed cranes that line the sky.
A myriad of them, poised to
lay new luxury flats abound.

Where pavements are now
the colour of corporate change:
industrial glass, industrial grey.

Community centres are shut
and the sound of children's play
drowned out by drilling and
cement mixing all day.

I used to see the soul
skipping round stall holders
dancing with buskers –
I see her now clinging

for dear life on a barren tree,
holding on to stumps
where leaves used to be.

I see her next lop-sided in the gutter
of this once heaving marketplace,
now tourist trap awash with
memorabilia and union jacks
or bustling shops shapeshifted into vacant lots.

I ask the soul what might be the matter.
She says in a cold, clear voice:

You cannot refurbish a street
and forget its soul
still looking
for a place to land.

Remi Graves writes:
Returning home after having been abroad for a while made me
see my area in a new light. It's changing in many ways, lots of luxury
flats are being built whilst shops are closing down. It got me thinking
about what happens to the soul of a place experiencing change,
and I started imagining a soul flying around, looking for a new place
to call home in its own area.

Paul Laurence Dunbar's poem is initially striking because of its song-like rhythm – whilst it's written in 'African American' dialect that might not be totally familiar, the rhythm and sentiment means you still understand the scenes being described. It's also interesting how the poem circles around the notion of spring (usually a pleasant shift in weather) which here is a nuisance to the speaker, whom we discover in the final stanza is a slave. I like the subtle way the poem sheds light on and subverts the usual 'the beauty of spring' style of poem, and presents us with a different view. The personification of animals adds an ironically nice light touch to a poem which also harbours some darker elements about America's history.

Spring Fever

Grass commence a–comin'
Thoo de thawin' groun',
Evah bird dat whistles
Keepin' noise erroun';
Cain't sleep in de mo'nin',
Case befo' it's light
Bluebird an' de robin,
Done begun to fight.

Bluebird sass de robin,
Robin sass him back,
Den de bluebird scol' him
'Twell his face is black.
Would n' min' de quoilin'
All de mo'nin' long,
'Cept it wakes me early,
Case hit's done in song.

Anybody wo'kin'
Wants to sleep ez late
Ez de folks 'll 'low him,
An' I wish to state
(Co'se dis ain't to scattah,
But 'twix' me an' you),
I could stan' de bedclothes,
Kin' o' latah, too.

'T ain't my natchul feelin',
Dis hyeah mopin' spell.
I stan's early risin'
Mos'ly moughty well;
But de ve'y minute,
I feel Ap'il's heat,
Bless yo' soul, de bedclothes
Nevah seemed so sweet.

Mastah, he's a–scol'in',
Case de han's is slow,
All de hosses balkin',
Jes' cain't mek 'em go.
Don' know whut's de mattah,
Hit's a funny t'ing,
Less'n hit 's de fevah
Dat you gits in spring.

Paul Laurence Dunbar (1872-1906)

Sophie Herxheimer

English Summer

Saturday till Tuesday
the window banged and thundered
gave us square panes of rain
like a still-wet painting of despair.
Stair-rods, said Gran.

Mum looked at the row of robot clouds
on her phone in her well-earned holiday hand.
It's going to brighten up! she perked.
No such thing as bad weather anyway,
added Gran, lying.

We pulled on wellies and braved the lane
the lump of clay-dark sky began to shift
then shred, surrender into small white rags
so sweet! No whiff of hostility...
Look at all that blue! marvelled Gran.

A row of blobby uneven puddles gleamed
visions of polished upside down
holiday clouds and houses, scribbled
with black lines, green daubs from trees.
Sunny again tomorrow! smiled Mum.

Sophie Herxheimer writes:

At first I found the theme 'Change' rather too huge to think about, then as I was walking around wondering what to write, I couldn't help noticing the incredible flashes of brilliant light in the park, following the rain. The wonderful blue of sky reflected in dingy puddles.

The changeability of our weather is one of the things I really enjoy. It's like having stage lighting and special effects for moods and feelings, especially when there are so many chances for a mismatch: like feeling cheerful on a sleety afternoon, or tired and wistful on a spring morning... I thought it would be fun to write about my puddle observation, and also the disappointment of a wet holiday... I wanted to put in the voice of experience (Gran) and the voice of hope (Mum) as well as the dominating reality, lashing rain for at least the first three days of a Devon holiday! I also wanted to contrast the predictable nature of a phone screen with its monotonous digital clouds on the weather forecast app, with being outdoors in actual reality where the clouds and every other detail are so fabulously varied.

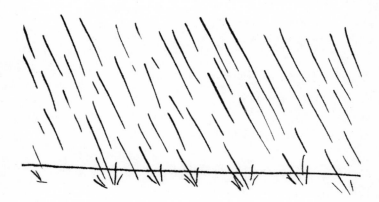

Why did I choose *The Sun and the Cloud* by Beata Duncan?

I like how this poet remembers her childhood experience of leaving her homeland and coming to England. When significant things occur in our lives, we may often recall the weather of that day or that period, and when similar weather occurs it may remind us of that big change we 'weathered'. The repetitions force the reader to go quite slowly in Beata Duncan's poem, as if you have to repeat the words and questions in order to make sense of them. Why can't she leave presents for her friends? Why is her teacher not quite so helpful? Why can't she finish her drawing?

The Sun and the Cloud

One day I was happy, running
to school with a book bag and pens,
the spring sun was shining
and my friends waiting.

There was a day
when the sun went into a cloud
my friends were a bit quiet
and I lost my book bag.

Another day the sun came out.
A girl just stared at me
as I ran up the stairs to join
my class. There was a cloud.

Our teacher wasn't quite so helpful.
I'm behind with my homework.
Never mind Mamma will be home,
she'll let me use her desk.

There was a day when Mamma said
It would be better I didn't go to school.
Why? I need to finish my story!
You can do that with me instead.

There was a day we all left.
I filled my bag as I was told.
Could I leave a present for my friends?
Pack your bags as you are told.

I watched the sun and the cloud.
I couldn't go to the park or my museum.
Could I leave a present for a friend?
Carry your bags as you are told.

There was a day we left.
The clouds covered the sun.
We must go, catch the train.
I want to finish my drawing.

Beata Duncan (1921-2015)

Michaela Morgan

Out of the Fire, a Spark

Out of the fire, a spark.
Out of the spark, a flame.
Out of the flame, a fire.
Change in a chain.

Out of the seed, a shoot.
Out of the shoot, a tree.
Out of the tree, a seed.
Change in a chain indeed.

From out of the raindrops, a puddle.
From out of the puddle, a cloud,
out of the cloud the rain.
Change again.

Out of the egg cracked a bird.
Out of the bird, a flap – and a fall.
Out of the fall, flight.
Change, that's right.

Out of the change, growth.
Out of the growth, change.
Growth, change; change, growth.
Change. Begin again.

Michaela Morgan writes:

I am moved by fairy tales, nursery rhymes, chants, folk song, folk dance, and by nature. I was aiming to have echoes of those in my poem – which could be performed by various voices in a chain. My poem is very simple and sees change as natural as growth.

Dover Beach is much more complex. In it, the poet Matthew Arnold is finding change unsettling. When he was writing (1867) it was a time of profound change in society and in thought, understanding, religion. The mood of this poem is melancholy and the poet, standing on the cliff by the deep sea, is edgy and anxious. He is clinging to the edge of his known reality and feeling threatened by the changes relentlessly lapping at him.

Dover Beach

The sea is calm tonight.
The tide is full, the moon lies fair
Upon the straits; on the French coast the light
Gleams and is gone; the cliffs of England stand,
Glimmering and vast, out in the tranquil bay.
Come to the window, sweet is the night-air!
Only, from the long line of spray
Where the sea meets the moon-blanched land,
Listen! you hear the grating roar
Of pebbles which the waves draw back, and fling,
At their return, up the high strand,
Begin, and cease, and then again begin,
With tremulous cadence slow, and bring
The eternal note of sadness in.

Sophocles long ago
Heard it on the Ægean, and it brought
Into his mind the turbid ebb and flow
Of human misery; we
Find also in the sound a thought,
Hearing it by this distant northern sea.

The Sea of Faith
Was once, too, at the full, and round earth's shore
Lay like the folds of a bright girdle furled.
But now I only hear
Its melancholy, long, withdrawing roar,
Retreating, to the breath
Of the night-wind, down the vast edges drear
And naked shingles of the world.

Ah, love, let us be true
To one another! for the world, which seems
To lie before us like a land of dreams,
So various, so beautiful, so new,
Hath really neither joy, nor love, nor light,
Nor certitude, nor peace, nor help for pain;
And we are here as on a darkling plain
Swept with confused alarms of struggle and flight,
Where ignorant armies clash by night.

Matthew Arnold (1822–1888)

Brian Moses

Fire

There was a fire in our house
when I was a boy,
a living, breathing family fire
that we'd sit in front of,
warming feet or hands
in cold weather.
We'd be blocking the heat
from the rest of the room
till Dad would say, "Let's feel
the warmth." Or if we forgot
to close the door he'd yell,
"Were you born in a barn?"
or, "Put the wood in the hole,
keep the heat in."
It was true what he said,
heat would leave through
an open door, and even a closed room
would have cold spots,
icy places where you never
felt warm at all.
There were compensations of course
in stories by the fire, figures
in the flames, shadows dancing

on the walls, muffins
held against the embers
till they toasted.
Nothing like that these days.
Coming home, coming in from
the street, to be met
by the warmth from radiators
with a cosy and safe sort of heat
that could never fuel
the imagination.

Brian Moses writes:
My childhood in the 1950s and 1960s is often a source of inspiration
for my poems. There is a huge difference between childhood today
and when I grew up. I remember how my house was always cold.
In the evening we'd all pull our chairs close to the fire with our dog
sprawled across the carpet in front of us. The open fire was a source

of magic, a place for stories and dancing shadows. A centrally heated house can only give us warmth. But would I go back to that era of chilblains and hot water bottles? Probably not!

Here is another poem to share with you. I chose *The Way Through the Woods* by Rudyard Kipling for two reasons. Firstly because it shows how something changes over time, and secondly because I happen to live in Burwash, which is the village where Rudyard Kipling lived for much of his later life.

The Way Through the Woods

They shut the road through the woods
Seventy years ago.
Weather and rain have undone it again,
And now you would never know
There was once a road through the woods
Before they planted the trees.
It is underneath the coppice and heath,
And the thin anemones.
Only the keeper sees
That, where the ring-dove broods,
And the badgers roll at ease,
There was once a road through the woods.
Yet, if you enter the woods

Of a summer evening late,
When the night-air cools on the trout-ringed pools
Where the otter whistles his mate,
(They fear not men in the woods,
Because they see so few.)
You will hear the beat of a horse's feet,
And the swish of a skirt in the dew,
Steadily cantering through
The misty solitudes,
As though they perfectly knew
The old lost road through the woods.
But there is no road through the woods.

Rudyard Kipling (1865-1936)

Cheryl Moskowitz

The Algonquin Calendar of Changing Moons

Dark nights growing

Wolf Moon
Snow Moon
Worm Moon

Nobody likes me

Buds start showing

Pink Moon
Flower Moon
Strawberry Moon

Served with cream and a silver spoon

Warm sun glowing

Buck Moon
Sturgeon Moon
Harvest Moon

Last one home's a pumpkin!

Leaves are blowing

Hunter's Moon
Beaver Moon
Cold Moon

When the year ends will you still be my friend?

Love bestowing

My Moon
Your Moon
Blue Moon

Round the earth and back again

Cheryl Moskowitz writes:
Like most poets I am drawn to big questions, *Why are we here?*
and *How do we become who we become?* I have always been
fascinated by the night sky and especially the moon, which always
appears to be so changeable, like people. Although the world is a
huge place I like the fact that wherever people are in the world and
whoever they are, we are all looking, and wondering, at the same
moon under the same sky. The Algonquin are a Native American
people who have given a separate name to each full moon that
occurs throughout the year. The names of the moons themselves are
like a poem.

Mary Lamb was an English poet who lived from 1764 until 1847.
Throughout her life Mary suffered from bouts of mental illness which

caused her, and her family, extreme distress. But despite this it seems Mary never wished that she could change hers for a different life, or be someone else. In a letter she wrote to her friend, Sarah Stoddart in 1803 Mary said, "...*I do not expect or want you to be otherwise than you are, I love you for the good that is in you, and look for no change.*" I find this poem of Mary's very moving. It tells us, I think, that we cannot change the person we are. The real change comes from discovering your own true value.

Envy

This rose-tree is not made to bear
The violet blue, nor lily fair,
   Nor the sweet mignionet:
And if this tree were discontent,
Or wished to change its natural bent,
   It all in vain would fret.

And should it fret, you would suppose
It ne'er had seen its own red rose,
   Nor after gentle shower
Had ever smelled its rose's scent,
Or it could ne'er be discontent
   With its own pretty flower.

Like such a blind and senseless tree
As I've imagined this to be,
   All envious persons are:
With care and culture all may find
Some pretty flower in their own mind,
   Some talent that is rare.

Mary Lamb (1764-1847)

Abigail Parry

Instructions for Not Becoming a Werewolf

You feel it first
as an itch in the teeth, a gnarl
of nerves coiled too tight.
Some taut aperture sliding open
between the heart and gut.
Precautions must be taken.

Do not enjoy too much
the quick grey jolt of hare, the split-crate thrill
of punctured appleskin.
High lonely places, wind,
the supple creak
of oiled leather. Woods

are of course best avoided.
Copses, spinneys, anywhere,
in fact, where the strong-sweet bulk of horse chestnut
crowds too close, where you can raise
the wet note of fresh-churned earth
by digging in the nails. Rivers

are not to be trusted. They know too much.
They nuzzle the base of cliffs and snout
at kitchen doors. They learn

from the granite of the hills, the pulp
of slick black roots and lovely braids
unwinding in the weeds. The moon

may be looked at in moderation.
But don't let it give you any ideas.

Fill your house with mirrors. Watch the clock.
Speak often. Do not feel
you are safe in the city: there's another
under this one. Stop your ears
to curlews, vixens, hounds, they've tales to tell

if you've the ears. And you've no idea
what it is to have ears like mine.

Abigail Parry writes:
I thought it would be public-spirited to pass on these instructions: by
following them, the sensible reader can hope to avoid this tiresome
condition. Ideally, you should refrain from going outside altogether,
and you should certainly not concern yourself with crows or conkers
or slowworms or stones with holes through the middle of them.
Otherwise you'll be letting yourself in for all sorts of nonsense.

If you ask people what they know about William Butler Yeats, they will probably tell you that he was Irish, or that he wore a very small pair of glasses, or perhaps that he was one of the most important poets of the twentieth century. They will probably not tell you that he was a werewolf but he gives himself away in this poem.

He mourns for the Change that has come upon him and his Beloved, and longs for the End of the World

Do you not hear me calling, white deer with no horns?
I have been changed to a hound with one red ear;
I have been in the Path of Stones and the Wood of Thorns,
For somebody hid hatred and hope and desire and fear
Under my feet that they follow you night and day.
A man with a hazel wand came without sound;
He changed me suddenly; I was looking another way;
And now my calling is but the calling of a hound;
And Time and Birth and Change are hurrying by.
I would that the Boar without bristles had come from the West
And had rooted the sun and moon and stars out of the sky
And lay in the darkness, grunting, and turning to his rest.

William Butler Yeats (1865–1939)

Rachel Piercey

Poor Pluto

Plenty of people presume: *Poor Pluto!*
Poor Pluto was just politely pacing
round the piping-hot sun
when it was promptly packed off
from the planetary party:
too piddly and powerless!
Poor Pluto, people pronounce,
praised as a planet
then plucked from position!
What a pride-popping pity.

But Pluto protests: *Please!*
Don't pour pessimism on me!
I am pottering at peace.
I prefer it parky,
and this pirouette of polar pieces
is my own private party.
I still parade past the pulsing sun.
I still perceive the pointed stars
on their patterned perches in the pitch.
Not a planet: not a problem. Being Pluto is perfect.

Rachel Piercey writes:

I co-edited an anthology of space poems a couple of years ago, and I have enjoyed researching and writing on the subject ever since. I always knew that I wanted to write about Pluto, which was discovered and named as the ninth planet in 1930, then reclassified as a dwarf planet in 2006. Throughout the 1990s, lots of other objects of similar and even greater size were discovered, and eventually the International Astronomical Union decided that Pluto did not count as a planet.

At first, I thought my poem was going to explore how Pluto might feel left out by this change in status – but when I started, I realised that Pluto wouldn't care at all! It still gets to turn around the sun and look at the stars, and it makes absolutely no difference which label those alien humans decide to use. I had fun thinking of words beginning with 'p' to create my alliterative poem, and it's very satisfying (if a little tongue-twisting) to read out loud.

Reading this poem by Edith Nesbit makes me feel like the sun has come out – it's so warm and colourful. Spring is my favourite season of all, and I love how the poem makes it into a special, celebratory occasion. I also love how each tree has its own distinctive personality and appearance. I have recently learnt to identify all sorts of trees – including the ones in this poem! – by looking at their leaves, blossom, fruit, buds and bark, which makes me feel more deeply connected to the natural world and brings me a lot of happiness. So as well as being about the changing seasons, this poem also reminds me of a lovely change I chose to make myself.

Child's Song in Spring

The silver birch is a dainty lady,
She wears a satin gown;
The elm tree makes the old churchyard shady,
She will not live in town.

The English oak is a sturdy fellow,
He gets his green coat late;
The willow is smart in a suit of yellow,
While brown the beech trees wait.

Such a gay green gown God gives the larches –
As green as He is good!
The hazels hold up their arms for arches,
When Spring rides through the wood.

The chestnut's proud and the lilac's pretty,
The poplar's gentle and tall,
But the plane tree's kind to the poor dull city –
I love him best of all!

E. Nesbit (1858–1924)

Rachel Rooney

Advice from a Caterpillar

When I was egg, I too, clung onto leaf
in shaded safety, hidden underside.
And fastened by a pinprick of belief
I dared to dream I was a butterfly.

A hunger hatched. I ate the home I knew
then inched along the disappearing green.
In shedding every skin that I outgrew,
became a hundred times the size I'd been.

And now I'm spinning silk to fix my spot.
Outside remains. Inside I'm changing things.
This caterpillar's planning on the lot;
proboscis and antennae, four bright wings.

So keep on clinging on, my ovoid one.
For who you are has only just begun.

Rachel Rooney writes:
I wrote this poem after reading *Alice in Wonderland*, by Lewis Carroll.
In the book, a talking caterpillar gives his advice to Alice – but in my
poem the caterpillar is talking to its younger self, a tiny caterpillar
egg. It's a poem that offers hope to those who might be struggling
or wanting their life to change. It is written in sonnet form.

The additional poem I have chosen is *Caterpillar* by Christina Rossetti. It is a poem I remember reading as a child. I chose it because, like my poem, it deals with the subject of a caterpillar's transformation into a butterfly. Here, the poet directly addresses the caterpillar, encouraging it on its journey. I particularly like the way Rossetti alternates the lines between long and short, mimicking the movement of a caterpillar as it stretches out then scrunches up.

Caterpillar

Brown and furry
Caterpillar in a hurry,
Take your walk
To the shady leaf, or stalk,
Or what not,
Which may be the chosen spot.
No toad spy you,
Hovering bird of prey pass by you;
Spin and die,
To live again a butterfly.

Christina Rossetti (1830–1894)

Joshua Seigal

The Both of Us

I used to be a butterfly
but now I'm just a slug.
I used to be a toothy grin
but now I'm just a shrug.
I used to be a rainforest
but now I'm just a tree.
It used to be the both of us
but now it's only me.

I used to be an estuary
but now I'm just a brook.
I used to be a library
but now I'm just a book.
I used to be a sanctuary
but now I'm just a zoo.
It used to be the both of us
but now there isn't you.

I used to be a dinosaur
but now I'm just a mouse.
I used to be a cityscape
but now I'm just a house.
I used to be a bakery
but now I'm just a bun.
It used to be the both of us
but now there's only one.

I used to be a symphony
but now I'm just a note.
I used to be democracy
but now I'm just a vote.
I used to be Mount Everest
but now I'm just a stone.
It used to be the both of us
but now I'm all alone.

Joshua Seigal writes:
This poem derives from a well-known workshop format, in which
poets use the phrase 'I used to... but now...'. I used this format to
explore the themes of loss and loneliness and to create interesting
metaphors around them. The poem explores some of the painful
connotations of 'Change'.

I chose the companion poem, by Eliza Cook, because it serves as a reminder that, no matter how great and mighty things seem on earth, everything is beholden to the passage of time. There is therefore no such thing as permanence, which forces us to think very hard about how we spend the very short amount of time granted to us.

Song of Old Time

I wear not the purple of earth-born kings,
Nor the stately ermine of lordly things;
But monarch and courtier, though great they be,
Must fall from their glory and bend to me.
My sceptre is gemless; yet who can say
They will not come under its mighty sway?
Ye may learn who I am,- there's the passing chime,
And the dial to herald me, Old King Time!

Softly I creep, like a thief in the night,
After cheeks all blooming and eyes all light;
My steps are seen on the patriarch's brow,
In the deep-worn furrows and locks of snow.
Who laughs at my power? the young and the gay;
But they dream not how closely I track their way.
Wait till their first bright sands have run,
And they will not smile at what Time hath done.

I eat through treasures with moth and rust;
I lay the gorgeous palace in dust;
I make the shell-proof tower my own,
And break the battlement, stone from stone.
Work on at your cities and temples, proud man,
Build high as ye may, and strong as ye can;
But the marble shall crumble, the pillar shall fall,
And Time, Old Time, will be king after all.

Eliza Cook (1818–1889)

Roger Stevens

Changing the Way You Read

Roger Stevens writes:
I'm busy compiling a book of riddles and puzzles and so I've
become very interested in how the reader sometimes has to change
his or her perception of a poem or verse for the puzzle to be solved.
Here are two poem-riddles. Can you solve them?

Hay.

Did Al? Did Al?

Thick hat

And thief hid Al

Dick owl chum pet

Offered immune

Deli dulled oggle aft

Oozy suds fun

Andy Dee

Shhh, Rhonda

Weigh whiff

Tea spoon

This poem first appeared in print in 1765 and no one has ever agreed
what it means. The truth is that it was found in an alien spacecraft
that had crash-landed on Earth. Perhaps you can at least help
translate it?

This poem first appeared written down in a book called *Folk Lore* in 1889. No one knows who wrote it as, up until then, it had been passed on orally, that is to say by being told by one person to another. The subject of the poem isn't change itself. Rather, the reader has to make a change in the way the poem is read for it to make sense.

Puzzle

I saw a fishpond all on fire
I saw a house bow to a squire
I saw a parson twelve feet high
I saw a cottage near the sky
I saw a balloon made of lead
I saw a coffin drop down dead
I saw two sparrows run a race
I saw two horses making lace
I saw a girl just like a cat
I saw a kitten wear a hat
I saw a man who saw these too
And said, though strange, they all were true.

Traditional

Answers

In the first poem, that nonsense is actually a well-known nursery rhyme. Try saying it out loud.

In the second poem, you have to move the second half of each line, to the line above. *I saw a house all on fire, I saw a parson bow to a squire* and so on. I'm not quite sure where the fishpond in the first line has disappeared to – but this verse *was* written a very long time ago and it seems that nobody remembers.

Jon Stone

Devil Bird Anagrams

I'm thinking, as I sink in milky <u>sunlight</u>
that filters through the window in the <u>kitchen</u>,
I'd like to be the swirl of swifts that <u>chase</u>
each other through the sky on slender <u>threads</u>
which never stop unreeling from their <u>spool</u>.
And sleep has not quite lifted all her <u>veils</u> –
my wings are stubs that end in bony <u>elbow,</u>
so as the daylight ripens in the <u>trees</u>,
I sink back into dreaming. What a <u>thing</u>:

jousting with the wind, and jostling, <u>hustling</u>
through crowds of cloud that soften, fatten, <u>thi_en</u>.
We'd stab the air like pangs, like little <u>a_es</u>,
and leave it ruffled, dazed – a little <u>tr__ed</u> –
than sign our names invisibly in <u>l__s</u>
and caper onward, squealing for our <u>l_s</u>.
We'd never touch the roaring ground <u>b____</u> ,
but bank and swerve and veer and sharply <u>s__</u> ,
and ride the rising thermals when it's <u>_____</u>.

Jon Stone writes:
'Devil bird' is an old folk name for the swift, whose arrival in Britain
signals the shift into summer. Flocks of them zipping around look
like letters assembling and disassembling on the sky's paper. I've
wondered what it would be like to change into not one single
swift, but dozens at once – the way a word or a sentence is,

paradoxically, one thing and also a collection of smaller things. It seemed to make sense, then, to write a poem that was also a word puzzle. Take the last word of each line apart, let the letters swoop around one another, and then reform them to get another word that fits into the second stanza. Sometimes it isn't the thing itself that changes, but how you perceive it.

I have chosen another poem to share with you ...
Sidney Keyes, who died in the Second World War when he was
just 20, often wrote about death. Here he addresses a different,
more gradual kind of change, one that he would never himself
experience. It's not a forlorn poem – there's something oddly
jubilant, oddly defiant about the elderly plowman being pals
with only the weeds, the seasons and the 'cold crazy moon'.

Plowman

Time was I was a plowman driving
Hard furrows, never resting, under the moon
Or in the frostbound bright-eyes morning
Labouring still; my team sleek-hided
As mulberry leaves, my team my best delight
After the sidelong blade my hero,
My iron-shod horses, my heroic walkers,
Now all that's finished.   Rain's fallen now
Smudging my furrows, the comfortable
Elms are windpicked and harbour now no singer
Or southward homing bird; my horses grazing
Impossible mountain-sides, long-frogged and lonely,
And I'm gone on the roads, a peevish man
Contending with the landscape, arguing
With shrike and shrewmouse and my face in puddles;
A tiresome man not listened to nor housed
By the wise housewife, not kissed nor handled
By any but wild weeds and summer winds,
Time was I was a fine strong fellow
Followed by girls. Now I keep company
Only with seasons and the cold crazy moon.

Sidney Keyes (1922-1943)

Kate Wakeling

Shadow Boy

Shadow boy's as shy as they come.
Dark as charcoal,
thin as air,
he tiptoes at the heels of his friends,
or lingers
patiently
under trees,
behind the wall,
at the base of a lamppost,
hoping to catch
a friendly foot.

Shadow boy's as shy as they come.
He tries his best
to brave the dark,
daring
to grow taller
and taller
as the sun sets.
But come the night,
shy shadow boy can only fade
then wait
until the bright dawn breaks.

Kate Wakeling writes:

I have always been interested in shadows. I love the mixture of science and stories that they hold: the way shadows are such a simple physical fact of life on earth, and yet they have such a mysterious charge too. I wrote *Shadow Boy* while thinking about what it would be like to be a shadow. I realised how strange and disquieting it must feel to be so entirely dependent on other forms and to find oneself growing then shrinking across each day. And so rather than dwelling on the menace often attributed to 'shadowy things', I wondered if shadows might instead be gentle, shy and full of longing.

Interim

The earth is motionless
And poised in space ...
A great bird resting in its flight
Between the alleys of the stars.
It is the wind's hour off ....
The wind has nestled down among the corn ....
The two speak privately together,
Awaiting the whirr of wings.

Lola Ridge (1873-1941)

Lola Ridge was a wild and courageous visionary who campaigned furiously for workers' rights and gender equality. She also wrote and published a number of poems. Her work receives relatively little airtime these days though, so it is a pleasure and honour to set this particular poem of hers loose here. *Interim* feels to me like a depiction of the world on the brink of change, perhaps the sort of change that Ridge fought and hoped for across her life. The 'whirr of wings' in the poem's last line is so full of energy and possibility, and reminds me of Ridge's own tireless work to improve the state of the world around her.

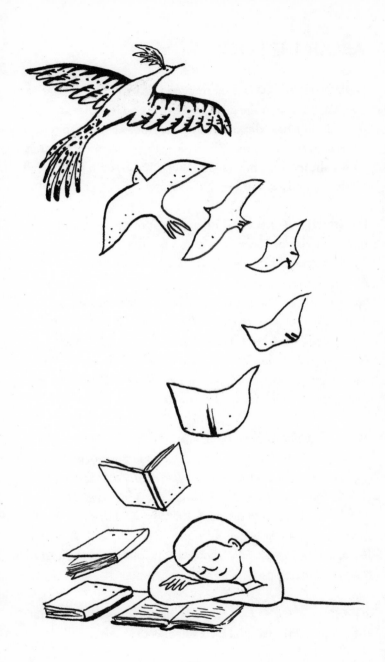

ABOUT THE POETS

Deborah Alma is the Emergency Poet in her vintage ambulance, which she takes to schools and libraries and festivals. She has edited three poetry books and written her own collection of poems too. She lives with her partner, the poet James Sheard, on a hillside in Powys, Wales, with a cat called Little My and a sheepdog called Daisy.

Liz Brownlee lives in the south west of England and visits schools accompanied by her assistance dog Lola. Liz is a poet, children's poet and film-maker. She has worked extensively with National Poetry Day and her series of film poems for NPD 2015 are available on her YouTube channel. Her books include *Animal Magic* and *Reaching the Stars, Poems about Extraordinary Women and Girls* (written with Jan Dean and Michaela Morgan). *The Same Inside* (written with Matt Goodfellow and Roger Stevens), and *Apes to Zebras, an A-Z of Shape Poems* (written with Sue Hardy-Dawson and Roger Stevens).

John Canfield grew up in Cornwall and now lives in London and works at The Poetry School. His poems have appeared in *Watcher of the Skies: Poems about Space and Aliens* and *Falling Out of the Sky: Poems about Myths and Monsters*, which was shortlisted for the CLiPPA award in 2016. He also runs writing and storytelling workshops in schools and for the Royal Opera House. His favourite type of change is the kind he can spend on crisps.

Joseph Coelho's poems have been published in several anthologies. His debut children's collection *Werewolf Club Rules* was the winner of the 2015 CLiPPA award. His collection for older readers, *Overheard In A Tower Block,* was longlisted for the 2018 Carnegie Medal. As well as poetry Joseph also writes picture books like *Luna Loves Library Day* and non-fiction books like *How To Write Poems.* All of his work has poetry and an element of performance at its heart, making his festival and school sessions dynamic occasions.

Sally Crabtree was once a world-class gymnast and is now turning the poetry world upside down with her cartwheeling poems and colourful, quirky performances. She has been described as "Profoundly original – one of Britain's richest inventions " (Lars Gustafsson, nominated for the Nobel Prize in literature) due to her innovative approach to presenting poetry to wide and diverse audiences and some of her trade mark interactive installations include: *The Poetree; I'll Eat My Words* range of edible poetry; *Word M'art* featuring poems in a tin; *Phone a Poem*; *Poetry Bingo* and the *Sweetshop of Words.* In 2016 she won a national ACORP award for her 'Song on the Tamar Valley line' community project with GWR.

Jan Dean writes poems. Writing poems is wonderfully strange – like playing lucky dip with a barrel full of tigers, raspberry jellies and machine parts. She visits schools where she performs her poetry and then invites the students into her head to play at poem-making. Jan's head is full of weird stuff. Her latest book – written with Roger Stevens – is *The Penguin In Lost Property,* so Jan is currently taking the Lost Property Office into schools looking for the owners of the ocean, two odd eyeballs and an antler (while the penguin escapes to have a poetry adventure).

Marjorie Lotfi Gill's poems have been published in journals and anthologies in the UK and US and been performed on BBC Radio 4. Her pamphlet *Refuge*, poems about her childhood in revolutionary Iran, is published by Tapsalteerie Press. In 2017 she was commissioned by Enterprise Music Scotland to write *Pilgrim*, a sequence about migration between Iran and the US, and by the University of Edinburgh to write *Bridge*, a companion sequence about a woman's migration within Europe. Marjorie founded the Belonging Project, creative writing workshops and readings considering the experiences of refugees with over 1,500 participants. She is a founder and director of Open Book, a charity providing shared reading and creative writing groups within community settings across Scotland.

Chrissie Gittins has published five collections of poetry for children. Her first three were Poetry Book Society Choices for the Children's Poetry Bookshelf and two were shortlisted for the CLiPPA award. *Stars in Jars* (2014), her new and collected poems, was a Scottish Poetry Library Recommendation. Chrissie appeared on BBC Countryfile with her latest collection *Adder, Bluebell, Lobster* (2016). Her poems have been animated for CBeebies TV. Chrissie is featured on the Poetry Archive, and has read her children's poems at festivals including Hay, Edinburgh, StAnza, Shetland, West Cork, and in the Children's Room of the Poets House in New York. She is the 2018 judge for the Caterpillar Prize for poems written for children by adults.

Matt Goodfellow is a poet and primary school teacher from Manchester. His acclaimed debut collection, *Carry Me*

Away, was released in 2016 and his most recent collections are *The Same Inside*, written with Liz Brownlee and Roger Stevens, and *Chicken on the Roof.* He still spends two days a week working as a primary school teacher. On the other days he tours the UK, visiting schools, libraries and festivals to deliver high-energy, fun-filled poetry performances and workshops.

Remi Graves is a London-based poet and drummer. A Barbican Young Poet, her work can be found in publications such as *Skin Deep*, *Orlando Zine* and *NON Quarterly*. Her past projects include a residency at Croydon Library with Spine Festival and she also held the role of Digital Poet in Residence with 1215.Today and The Poetry School. Remi is a 2017–2018 Toast Poet.

Sophie Herxheimer is an artist, a poet and a terrific inspirer of poetry and art in others. Sophie trained in painting at Camberwell and Chelsea. She's held residencies for LIFT, Southbank Centre and Transport for London. Exhibitions include The Whitworth, The Poetry Library and The National Portrait Gallery. She has illustrated five fairy tale collections; made several artists' books; created a 300 metre tablecloth to run the length of Southwark Bridge, featuring hand printed food stories from a thousand Londoners; narrated an episode of *The Food Programme* from Margate; made a life size concrete poem in the shape of Mrs Beeton and a pie big enough for seven drama students to jump out of on the lawn of an old peoples' home. Recent publications include *The Listening Forest*, *The New Concrete* and most recently *Velkom to Inklandt*.

Michaela Morgan is a poet and writer. She has a collection of awards and shortlistings including the BBC Blue Peter Book Award. Sadly, she has lost her Blue Peter badge. Hundreds of her poems are scattered in anthologies in the UK and internationally. She edited *Alice in Poetry* (2016), an anthology providing poetic responses to *Alice in Wonderland,* and contributed to *Reaching the Stars: Poems about Extraordinary Women and Girls.* She regularly visits schools and runs workshops.

Brian Moses has been a children's poet since 1988. To date he has had over 200 books published. Brian also runs writing workshops and performs his own poetry and percussion shows. He has given over 3,000 performances in schools, libraries, theatres and at festivals throughout the UK and abroad. Recent books include: *Lost Magic: The Very Best of Brian Moses*, *The Waggiest Tails – Poems Written by dogs* with help from Brian Moses & Roger Stevens, *Beetle in the Bathroom,* a picture book, *I Thought I Heard a Tree Sneeze – a best of Brian's poems for younger children* (2018) and his first fiction title, *Python*.

Cheryl Moskowitz writes for adults and children. From 2014 to 2017 she pioneered a ground-breaking Poetry Residency working with pupils, staff and the wider community at Highfield Primary School, North London. Her poems for children have appeared in recent anthologies, *Is This a Poem?* edited by Roger Stevens, *Wonderland: Alice in Poetry* edited by Michaela Morgan and The Emma Press's *Watchers of the Skies*, edited by Rachel Piercey and Emma Wright. Other publications and broadcasts include *Poetry Pie*

(CBeebies), *Can It Be About Me?*, *Poetry at Highfield* and *The Girl is Smiling*.

Abigail Parry's poems have been set to music, translated into Spanish and Japanese, and tipped onto London from a helicopter. Her poems for children have appeared in anthologies of monsters and aliens, and she once dressed up as six different Aztec gods for one frenetic poetry reading. She has won a number of prizes and awards for her work, including the Ballymaloe Prize, the Troubadour Prize and an Eric Gregory Award. Her first collection, *Jinx*, is published by Bloodaxe.

Rachel Piercey is a freelance writer, editor and proofreader. She co-edited the children's poetry anthologies *Falling Out of the Sky: Poems about Myths and Monsters* and *Watcher of the Skies: Poems about Space and Aliens*, both published by the Emma Press; the former was shortlisted for the CLiPPA award in 2016. She has taught courses on writing poetry for children for The Poetry School, and regularly performs and runs poetry workshops in primary schools. Her poems for adults have been published in *The Rialto*, *Magma*, *Butcher's Dog* and *The Poetry Review*, as well as two Emma Press pamphlets and various anthologies.

Rachel Rooney's first poetry collection *The Language of Cat* won the CLPE Poetry Award and was long-listed for the Carnegie Medal. Her second collection *My Life as a Goldfish* was shortlisted for the CLiPPA 2015. Her newest collection is *A Kid in my Class,* illustrated by Chris Riddell. Rachel visits schools for workshops with pupils and has performed her work at festivals and for The Children's Bookshow. She was Chair of Judges for the CLiPPA 2017 and the Betjeman Poetry Prize.

Joshua Seigal is a poet, performer and workshop leader from London. He has poetry books published by Bloomsbury and children's picture books published by Flying Eye. He frequently visits schools around the country, and has been described by teachers as "inspirational" and "a positive male role model". Joshua has taken his one-man shows to the Edinburgh Festival Fringe, the Edinburgh Book Festival and the Cheltenham Literature Festival. His book *I Don't Like Poetry* was shortlisted for the 2017 Lollies Award.

Roger Stevens visits schools, libraries and festivals performing his work and running workshops for young people and teachers. He is a founding member of the Able Writers scheme with Brian Moses, and runs the award-winning poetry website www.poetryzone.co.uk for children and teachers. He has published nearly forty books of poetry for children. His most recent books are: *The Same Inside*, poems about empathy and friendship, with Liz Brownlee and Matt Goodfellow; *The Waggiest Tails, poems written by dogs*, with Brian Moses; and *Apes to Zebras,* a collection of Shape Poems, with Liz Brownlee and Sue Hardy-Dawson. Roger spends his time between his homes in central France and Brighton, where he lives with his wife and a very, very shy dog called Jasper.

Jon Stone was born in Derby and lives in London. His children's poems have previously been published in *Falling*

Out of the Sky (The Emma Press, 2015) and *Watcher of the Skies* (The Emma Press, 2016). His collection *School of Forgery* (Salt, 2012) was a Poetry Book Society recommendation, and was reprinted in paperback in 2018. He won an Eric Gregory Award in 2012 and the *Poetry London* Prize in both 2014 and 2016. As well as writing, he co-runs small press Sidekick Books with Kirsten Irving, publishing compendiums of visual, ecological and experimental poetry.

Kate Wakeling is a poet and musicologist. *Moon Juice*, her first collection for children, won the CLiPPA in 2017 and was nominated for the Carnegie Medal. A pamphlet of her poetry for adults, *The Rainbow Faults*, is published by The Rialto, and her poetry has appeared in magazines and anthologies including Magma, Oxford Poetry, the Guardian and *The Forward Book of Poetry* 2016.

READ POETRY FOR A CHANGE...

"Poetry literally breaks reading and writing into bite-sized chunks. It is a fun, non-threatening way for children to become more literate. In poetry sessions I've seen elective mutes stand up at the front of their class and read, been told by countless teachers that 'that student never normally puts pen to paper', watched children cry and laugh and think together."

Joseph Coelho, poet and National Poetry Day Ambassador

Every day can be poetry day, once you realise you can enjoy poetry anywhere. Change your life for the better: read poetry, read it aloud, perform it, write it.

Have a look at these activities designed to help you to get the most out of poetry. They're fun and simple to do either at school or as a family.

THINGS TO TALK ABOUT

What is poetry? What does it mean to you?
Ask people what they think poetry is – how would they describe it? What does poetry mean to them? Is it something that rhymes; or that doesn't have to rhyme? Is it funny, beautiful, boring? Does it help you feel or understand things?

Make a list and see how many different things poetry can be to different people. (Extra discussion point: football commentators and headline writers have been known to use the phrase "pure poetry" to describe a great goal or save. Why do you think they do that?)

What kinds of poetry do you know?
Make a list of all the different kinds of poetry people know – e.g. limericks, rap, haikus, nursery rhymes, free verse, story poems. Keep the list up for people to see, and add to it as they meet new kinds of poetry.

ONE WAY TO TALK ABOUT A POEM

When you share a poem together read it through more than once, maybe a few times. Make copies for others to read; ask people if they would like to read it aloud. Then get them talking about it, maybe by asking 'What lines do you like most in this poem?'

Make it clear that there is no right or wrong answer, nor is the poem a problem to be solved. Everyone will find their own meanings, likes and dislikes, and that makes for great discussion. Here are some more questions you could ask:

What do you think is the main thing being said in this poem? How does the poem make you feel? Why?

THINGS TO DO

Create a poem from words in a newspaper
Cut out words and phrases from newspapers and magazines. Spread them out to see what you've got, move them around and group them. What might you write a poem about? Arrange the cuttings to make a poem.

Reading aloud
Enjoy reading your favourite poems aloud and listening to each other reading. As you read and listen you'll find yet more meaning and pleasure. Choose your favourites from this book, or look out for longer story poems like *The Highwayman* (Alfred Noyes), *The Owl and the Pussycat* (Edward Lear) or *The Lady of Shalott* (Alfred Lord Tennyson).

Learning poetry off by heart
Learning to say or perform a poem aloud can be a great confidence builder, especially if there's a chance to try out other voices and become someone else. And it can indeed be 'by heart' – you'll get pleasure from the poetry, and a deeper understanding of the words – and you'll be able to share that pleasure with others.

A good way to learn by heart is in a group: choose a poem with strong metre and rhyme (much easier to learn than free verse) and put it up on the whiteboard. Ask the children to read it aloud a couple of times, then cover it up and see how much they can remember, a line at a time. Split the group and make it a competition.

WATCH POETS 'LIVE'

On video and film
Watch poets reading and talking about their work on the internet. Find and listen to your favourites, and get to know new ones. You'll find film clips on the National Poetry Day website but also visit CLPE too: *clpe.org.uk* or the Children's Poetry Archive
www.childrenspoetryarchive.org or *poetrystation.org.uk*

At a live event
Hearing a poet read aloud is fun and inspiring. On and around National Poetry Day, there are live poetry events taking place in all sorts of places, from libraries and bookshops to cafes and clubs. Find out what's happening near you by checking the events map on the National Poetry Day website, or signing up to the Poetry Library alerts. Or why not invite a poet to visit your school? You can contact poets direct, or go through agencies such as **Authors Aloud, Authors Abroad** and **Speaking of Books**. Find out more on their websites.

INSPIRATION WITH A FAVOURITE POEM

Here is a way of further enjoying a favourite poem – and then being inspired to write your own.

Write your own poem
Choose a poem from this book, and spend time reading it together and talking about it, including the context in which

it was written. Hide the title – and ask people what title they would give it. When you feel you're getting to know the poem, have a go at giving it a new first or last line. Or take the first line and then follow on by writing your own poem. This can be a powerful way of using the emotion of the original to write about your own feelings.

Acting out poems

Many poems work well in performance. Choose a poem, read and talk about it together, then divide it up so that children in twos or threes can work together on actions for their part of the poem.

The groups then come together and each group acts out their part. Give feedback to each other – say which parts worked well and suggest ideas for how it might be better, so that together you can shape up the whole performance.

MORE THINGS YOU CAN DO

There are lots more ideas for poetry activities, for both schools and families on the National Poetry Day website *www.nationalpoetryday.org*

ABOUT NATIONAL POETRY DAY

National Poetry Day takes place generally on the first Thursday in October and each year inspires people throughout the UK and beyond to enjoy, discover and share poems. Everyone is invited to join in, whether by organising events, displays, competitions or by simply posting favourite lines of poetry on social media using #nationalpoetryday.

THANKS AND ACKNOWLEDGEMENTS

This book owes its existence to the energy and vision of Andrea Reece, National Poetry Day's manager. She has been greatly helped by Holly Hopkins, manager of the Forward Prizes. Together with Susannah Herbert, they form the Forward Arts Foundation, a charity whose mission is to celebrate excellence in poetry and increase its audience.

Forward Arts Foundation is an Arts Council National Portfolio organisation, supported by the Esmée Fairbairn Foundation and the John Ellerman Foundation.